# FIGHTER PLANES

## CAVAN SCOTT

Badger Publishing Limited
Oldmedow Road,
Hardwick Industrial Estate,
King's Lynn PE30 4JJ
Telephone: 01438 791037

www.badgerlearning.co.uk

2 4 6 8 10 9 7 5 3 1

Fighter Planes ISBN 978-1-78464-016-3

Text © Cavan Scott 2014
Complete work © Badger Publishing Limited 2014

Publisher: Susan Ross
Senior Editor: Danny Pearson
Publishing Assistant: Claire Morgan
Designer: Fiona Grant
Series Consultant: Dee Reid

Photos: Cover Image: Paul Grover/REX
Page 5: Courtesy Everett Collection/REX
Page 6: © Anthony Kay/Flight/Alamy
Page 7: Roger Viollet/Getty Images
Page 8: © Aviation History Collection/Alamy
Page 9: Rupert Hartley/REX
Page 10: Associated Newspapers/Associ/REX
Page 11: Associated Newspapers/Associ/REX
Page 12: © Maurice Crooks/Alamy
Page 13: David Hartley/REX
Page 14: REX
Page 15: jeremkin/iStock Vectors/Getty Images
Page 16: REX
Page 17: Nicolas Messyasz/Sipa/REX
Page 19: REX
Page 20: Archive Photos/Getty Images
Page 21: Ted Blackbrow/REX
Page 22: Image Broker/REX
Page 23: Ian Black/REX
Page 24: © War Archive/Alamy
Page 26: Tom Stoddart/Getty Images
Page 28: REX
Page 30: Erik Simonsen/Getty Images

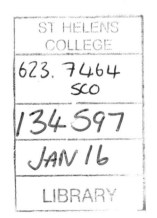

# Contents

## Vocabulary

aeroplanes

canopy

dogfight

parachute

propeller

radar

Royal Air Force

Sopwith Camel

# 1. DOGFIGHTS

The word 'dogfight' was first used during World War One to describe a fight between two aeroplanes.

Many aircraft where shot down by guns on the ground but the most dangerous battles took place in the sky.

World War One began in 1914.

At first, aeroplanes didn't take part in battles. They were just used to spy on the enemy or watch battles from the sky.

Then machine guns were fixed on the nose of fighter planes.

Dogfights were fought in the skies as fighter pilots tried to shoot each other down.

WOW! facts

Pilots who shot down five or more enemy aeroplanes were called 'Aces'.

## The Sopwith Camel

The Sopwith Camel was a 'biplane'. It had two sets of wings.

It could reach speeds of 115 miles per hour.

Can you guess why it was called a 'camel'?*

WOW! facts

Over 5400 Sopwith Camels were built during the World War One.

*A metal cover protecting the guns created a 'hump' at the front.

# 2. THE SECOND WORLD WAR

World War Two began in 1939.

Fighter aircraft now had only one set of wings, but they could reach speeds of over 300 miles per hour.

Pilots had to be protected from the wind by a canopy over the cockpit.

**The Battle of Britain**

The Battle of Britain is one of the most famous battles of World War Two.

It began in July 1940 when German aircraft started bombing British ships.

By August, German fighters were attacking the bases where the Royal Air Force planes were kept.

The Royal Air Force were outnumbered and outgunned, but they fought back.

By September, the Germans put off their plans to invade Britain.

The Battle of Britain had been won, but at great cost.

This wall shows the names of all the British servicemen and women who took part in the Battle of Britain.

During the Battle of Britain, the Royal Air Force lost around 1023 aircraft, while 1887 German aircraft were shot down.

**The Spitfire**

Over 20,000 Spitfire planes were produced between 1938 and 1948.

By the end of the war in 1945, Spitfires could fly at 440 miles per hour.

The aircraft's guns were fixed on its wings, and some Spitfires also carried bombs.

# 3. JET FIGHTERS

The Spitfire could fly four times as fast as the Sopwith Camel.

But 440 miles per hour was the maximum speed for a propeller aircraft.

You just couldn't make a propeller spin any faster.

But the Air Force wanted faster planes so planes were fitted with jet engines instead of propellers.

Jet engines burn fuel to spin the blades of a turbine.

This pushes an aircraft forwards like air escaping from a balloon. They can fly much faster than planes with propellers.

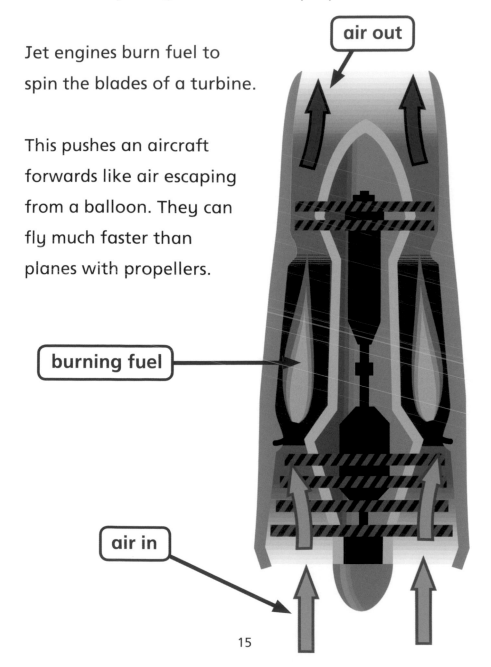

air out

burning fuel

air in

Jet fighters can also fly faster because their wings are swept back like an arrowhead.

Jet fighters can reach speeds of over 1300 miles per hour.

That's more than twice the speed of sound.

Dogfights have
become more
dangerous than ever.
Pilots need to make
split-second decisions.

Even the smallest mistake
can be fatal.

## F-22 Raptor

The F-22 Raptor is the most important fighter aircraft of the 21st Century.

Its jets swivel so that it can quickly change direction in the sky.

The fighter's design means it's almost impossible to see on radar too.

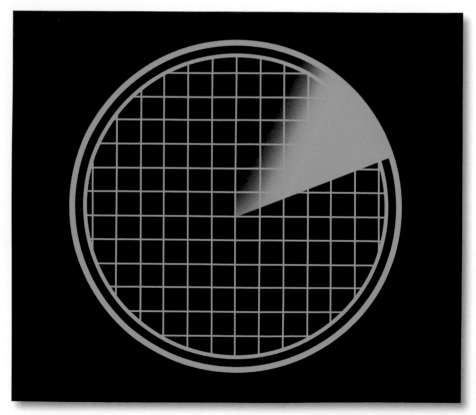

WOW! facts

Spitfires cost £6000 each.
F-22 Raptors can cost over
£60 million each!

# 4. CHANGING WEAPONS

### Early bombs

The first bombs on planes were just dropped out of the plane by hand!

In World War Two, bombs were dropped from racks under the aircraft.

## Machine guns

The first fighter planes needed machine guns that could fire through a propeller without shooting the blades off.

A gun was made that could be linked to the propeller so that it never hit the blades.

WOW! facts

Modern jet fighters can fire over 6000 rounds per minute.

## Sidewinder missiles

The United States Navy invented the first Sidewinders in 1953.

These missiles find their targets by locking onto the heat of an enemy's engine.

## Smart bombs

Smart bombs are dropped like regular bombs but then they can be guided to hit a target.

Sometimes they are guided by GPS. That's the same Global Positioning System that you find in a car's satnav!

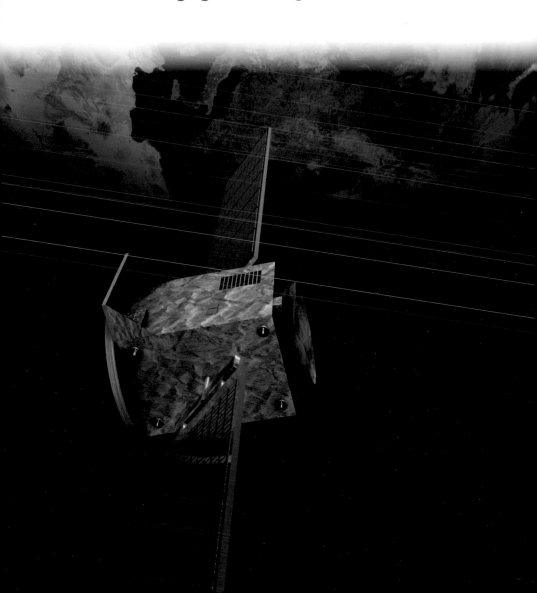

# 5. PILOTS THEN AND NOW

Over the last hundred years, the clothes pilots wear have changed almost as much as the planes they fly.

**Then**

Early pilots wore simple uniforms to protect them while flying.

1. Cockpits on planes like the Sopwith Camel had no canopies so pilots wore goggles to protect their eyes.

2. Pilots spent a lot of time turning to see if enemy fighters were on their tail. Pilots often wore silk scarves to stop their necks rubbing against their collars. They also used their scarves to wipe grease from their goggles.

3. Pilots wore long leather flying jackets over their uniforms to keep them warm. They also wore leather hats lined with warm wool, and long leather gloves.

Early fighter pilots didn't wear parachutes. They were too bulky to fit in the cockpit!

## Now

Today's pilots wear high-tech clothes to keep them safe.

1. A lightweight but strong helmet protects the pilot's head from being bashed. The helmets are nicknamed 'bone domes'! The visor protects the pilot's eyes from sudden flashes and sunlight.

2. Pilots wear special headphones to protect their ears from the roar of the engines.

3. Oxygen masks provide an air supply when flying at great heights.

4. Pilots wear an all-in-one flight suit, which is light to wear and fire-proof.

If a plane is in trouble, pilots can blast themselves clear using a rocket-powered ejector seat. The parachute is automatically pulled when the seat is at a safe distance.

# 6. FIGHTER PLANES OF THE FUTURE

In the future, fighter aircraft may not have pilots at all. Unmanned aircraft are already used in many war zones around the world.

Unmanned aircraft are known as drones. They can be controlled remotely or even by computer.

Because there is no pilot on board, drones can be smaller and lighter than normal fighter aircraft.

In the future, drones will be able to fly faster too.

The United States Air Force is already testing an unmanned aircraft called the Falcon HTV-2 that could reach speeds of 13,000 miles per hour.

| Form of travel | Time to travel the distance from London to Sydney, Australia |
| --- | --- |
| boat | 32-40 days |
| Jumbo jet | 23 hours |
| Falcon HTV-2 | 49 minutes |

13,000 miles per hour is
20 times the speed of sound.
That's fast!

But what weapons will you find in the fighter aircraft of the future?

By 2030, the US Air Force plans to have fighter planes armed with laser beams rather than missiles!

The dogfights of the future may be more like something out of a science fiction film.

## Questions

What does 'dogfight' mean? *(page 5)*

How does the Sopwith Camel get its name? *(page 8)*

When did World War Two begin? *(page 9)*

Who lost more aircraft in the Battle of Britain – Britain or Germany? *(page 12)*

How much does an F-22 Raptor cost? *(page 19)*

Name one thing a modern pilot wears in the air. *(page 27)*

# INDEX